How to Draw Cartoon Owls

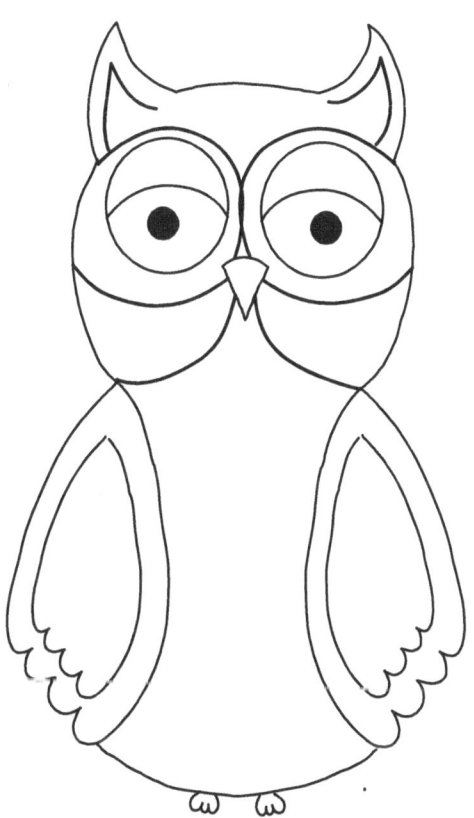

Designed and Illustrated by Beth Ingrias

Copyright 2017 Team of Light Media LLC
All Rights Reserved
ISBN-13: 978-1979200967
ISBN-10: 1979200963

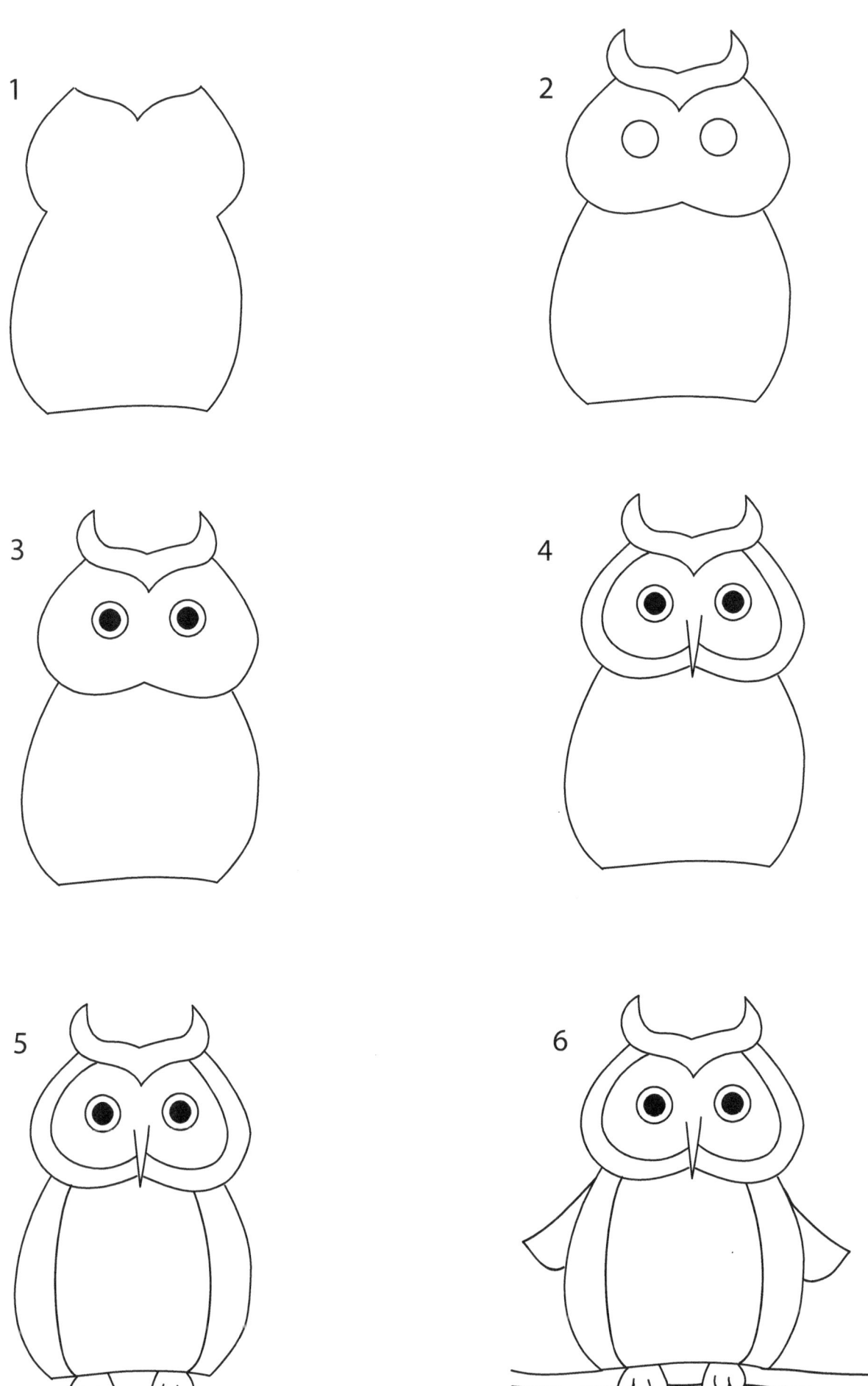

Practice Page

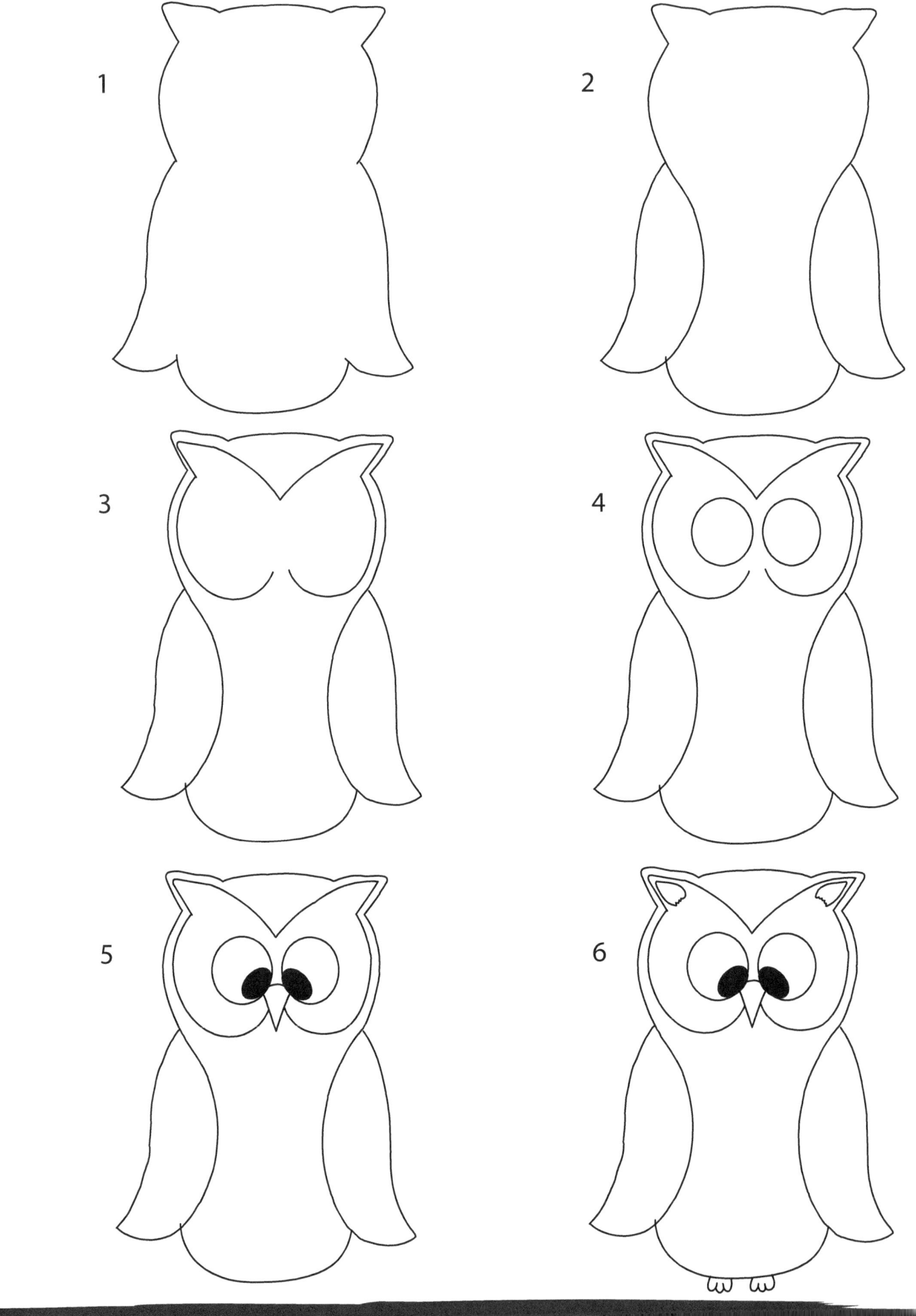

Practice Page

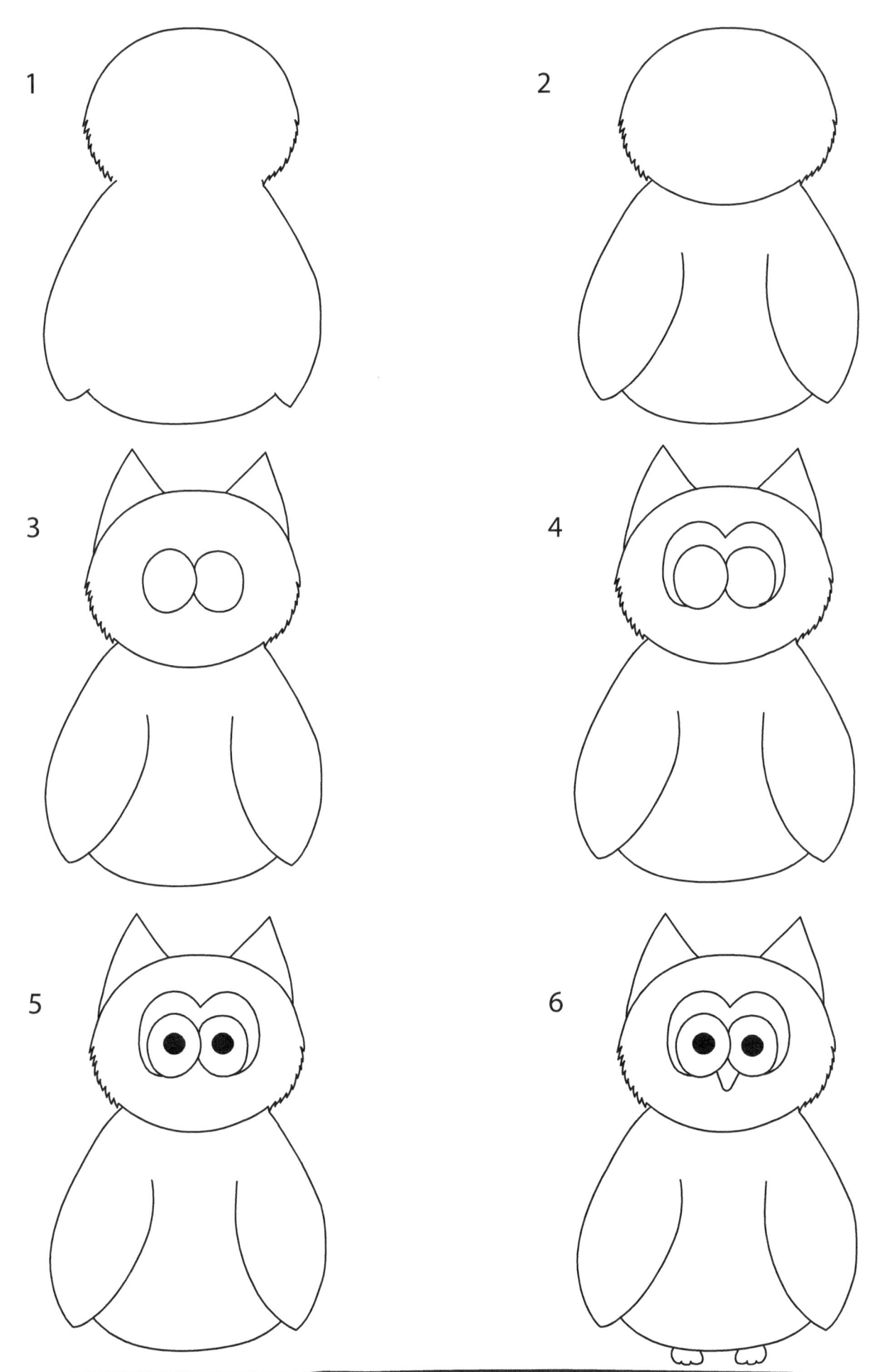

Practice Page

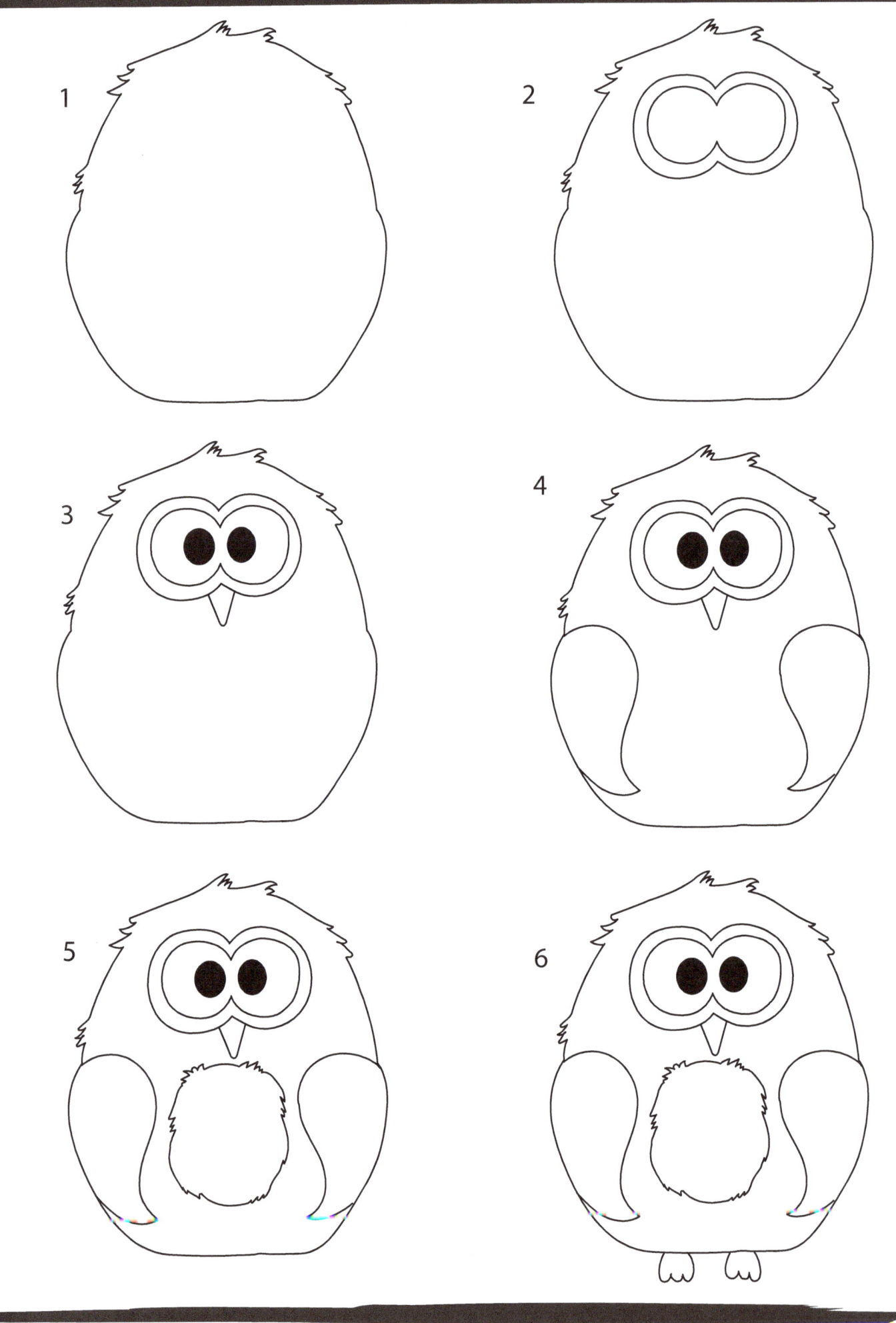

Practice Page

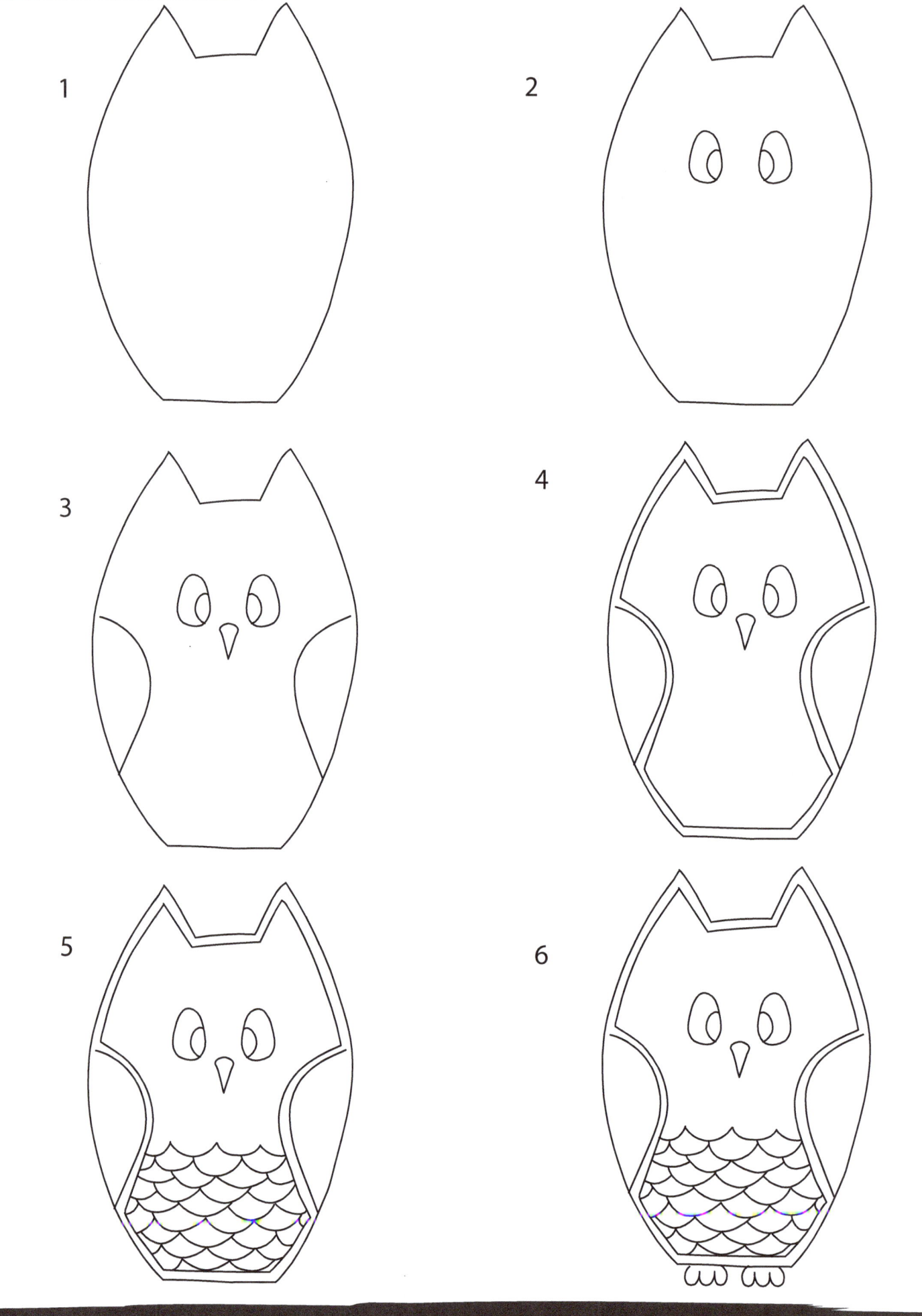

Practice Page

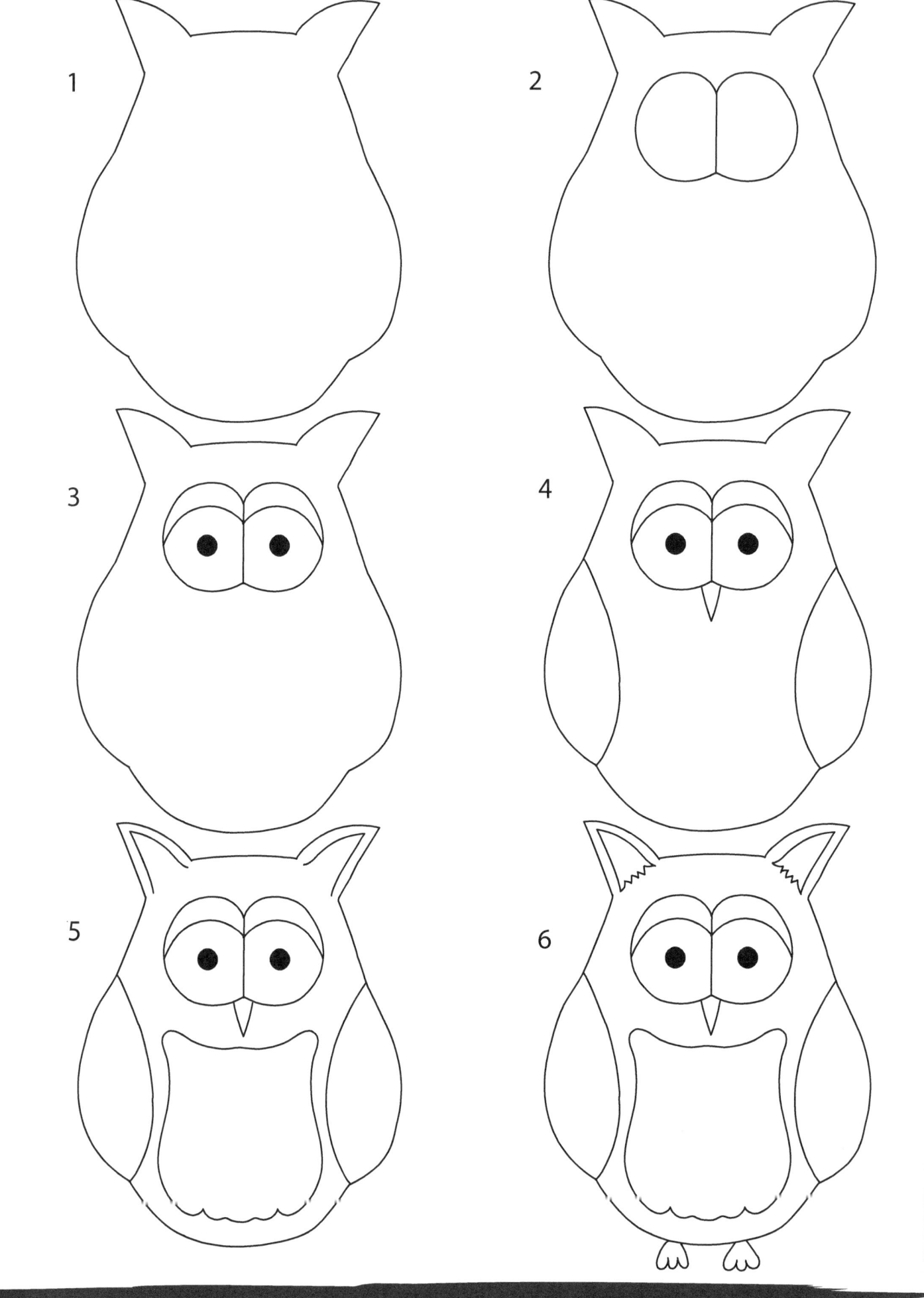

Practice Page

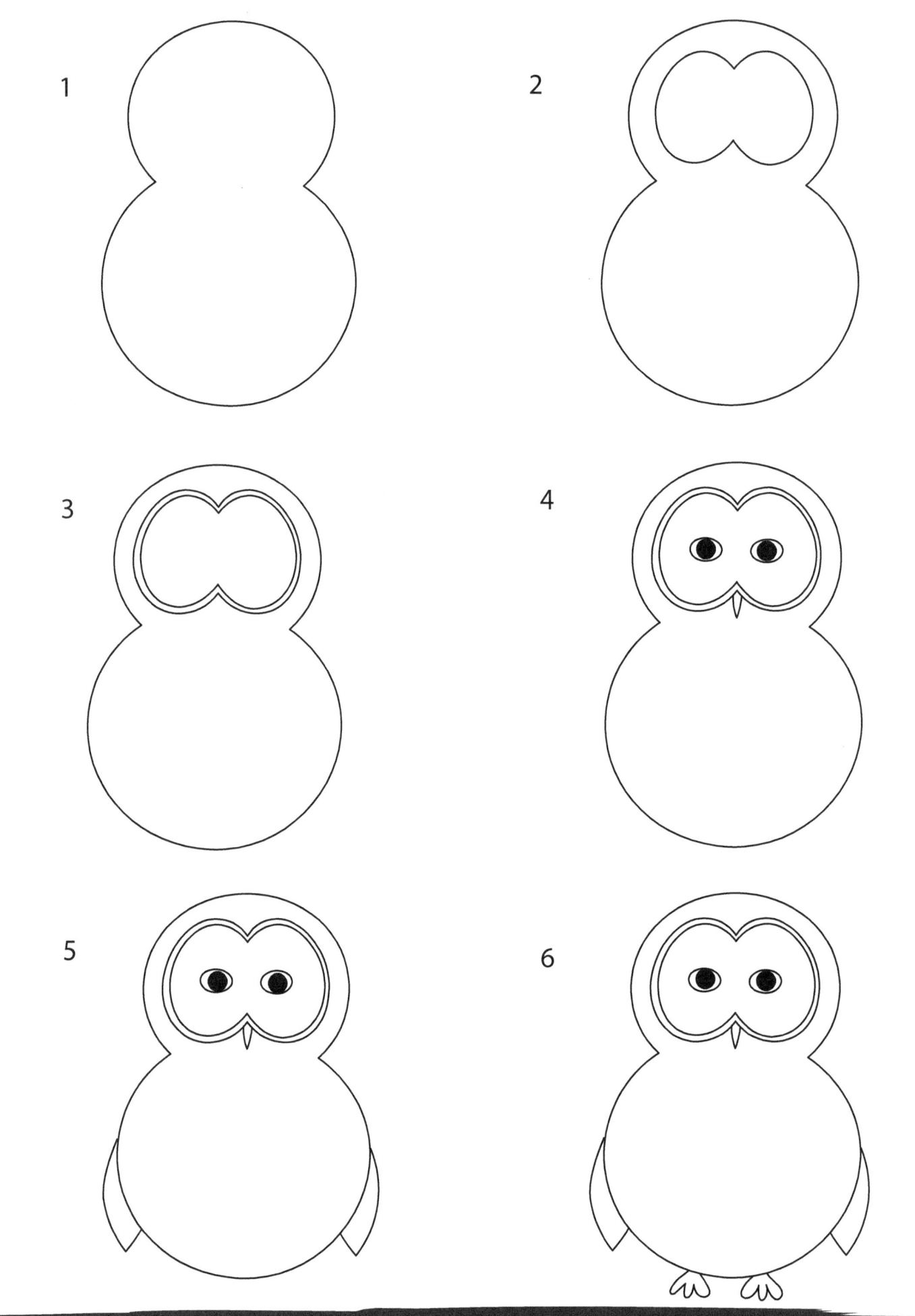

Practice Page

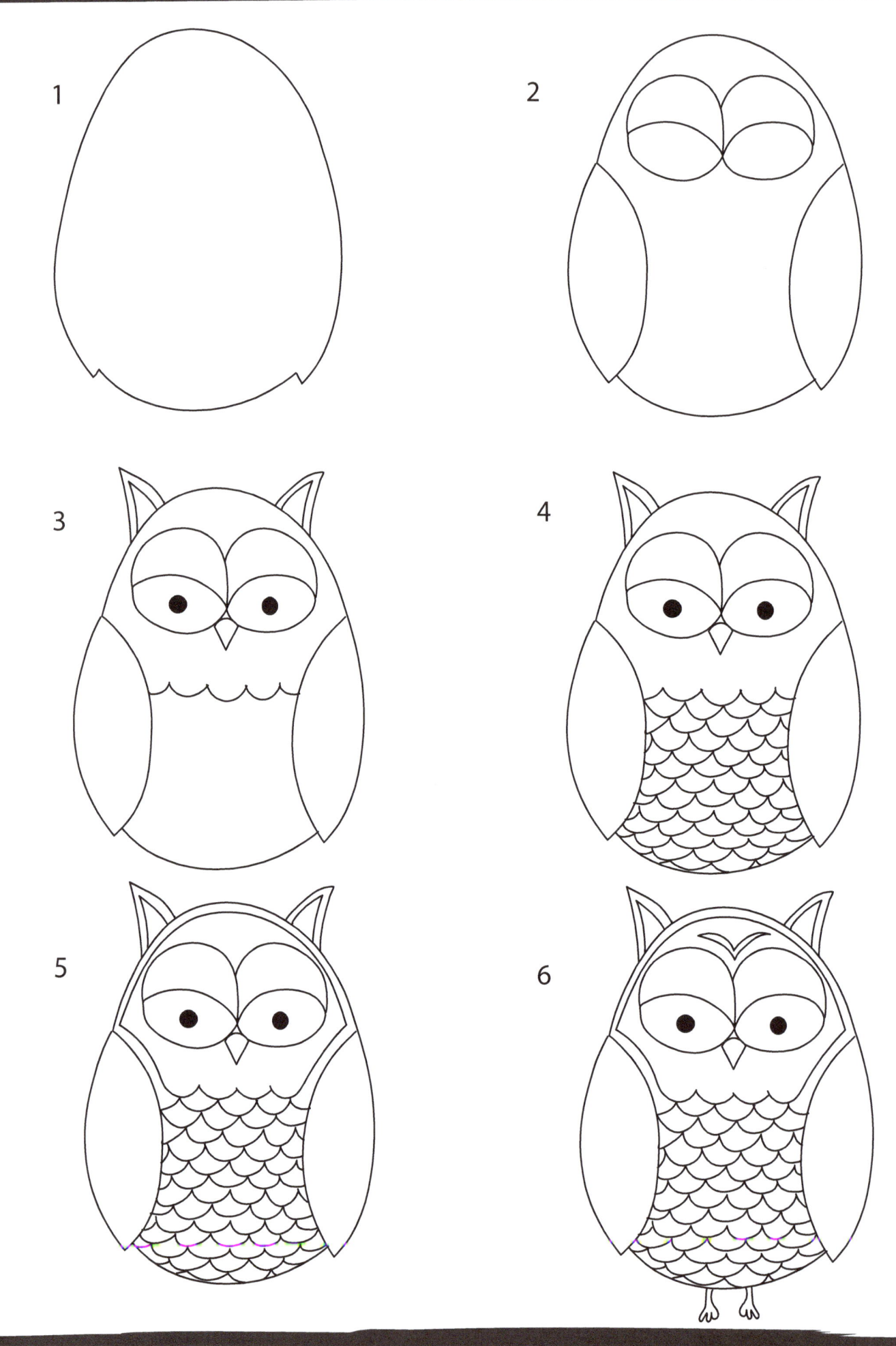

Practice Page

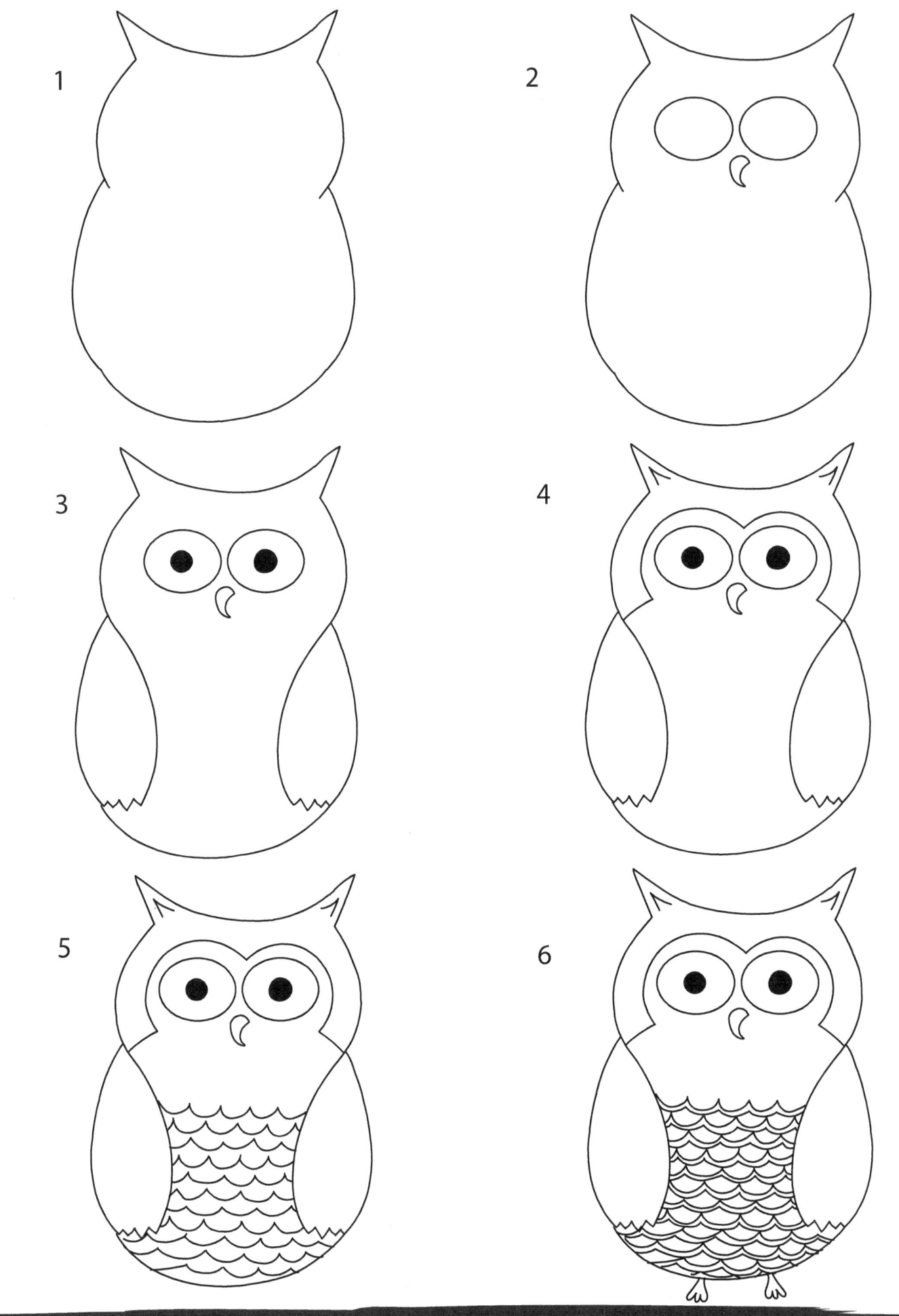

Practice Page

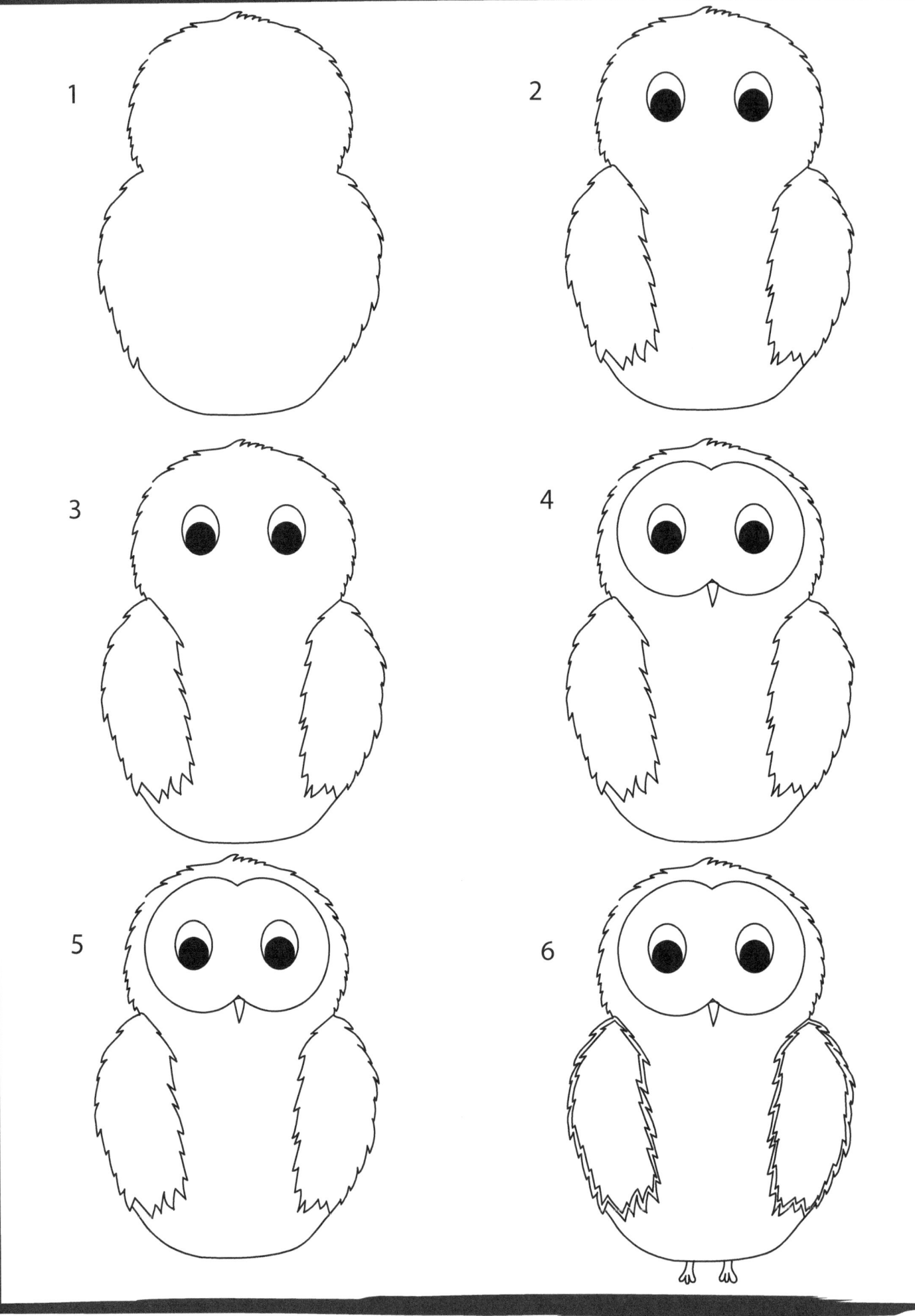

Practice Page

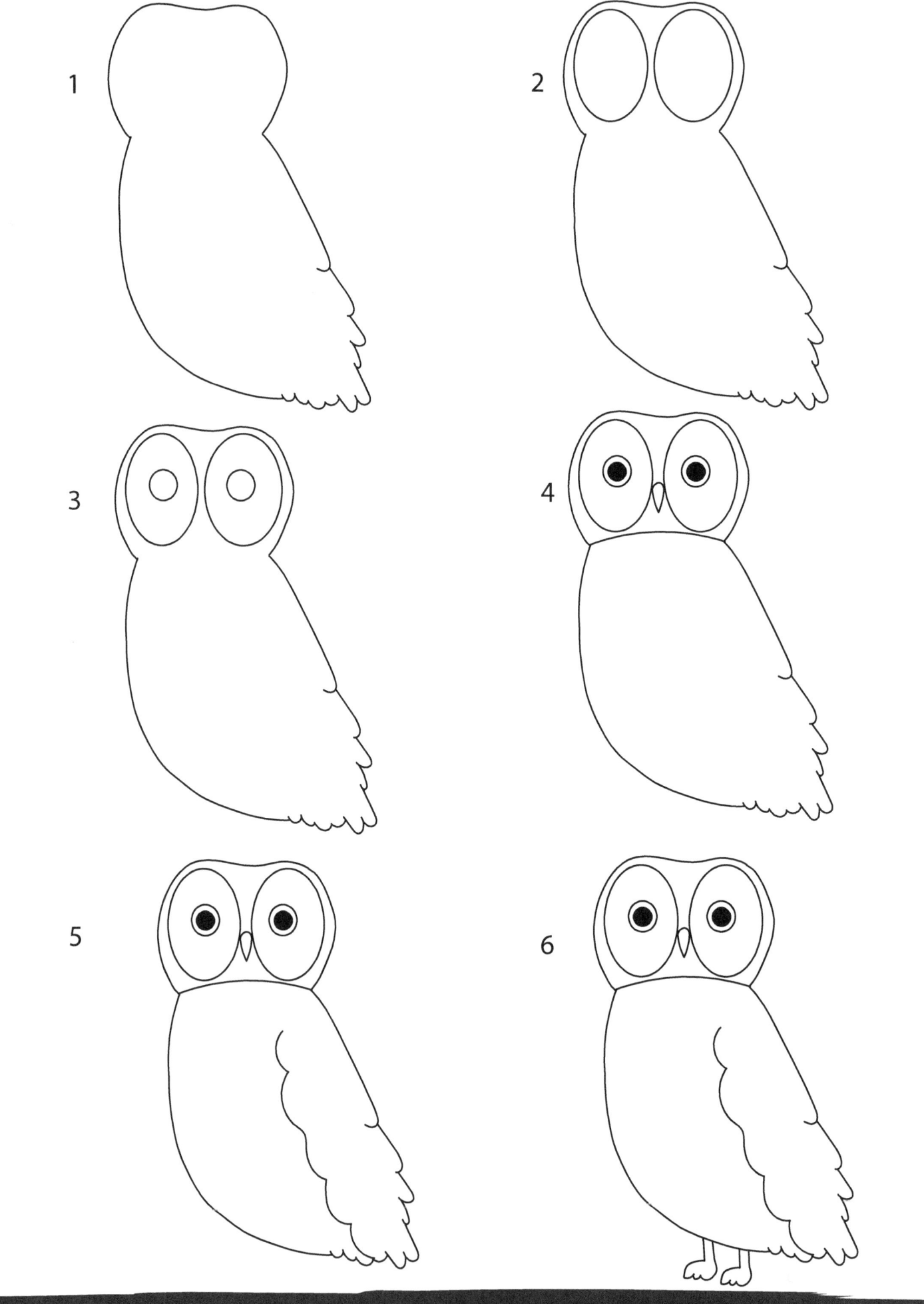

Practice Page

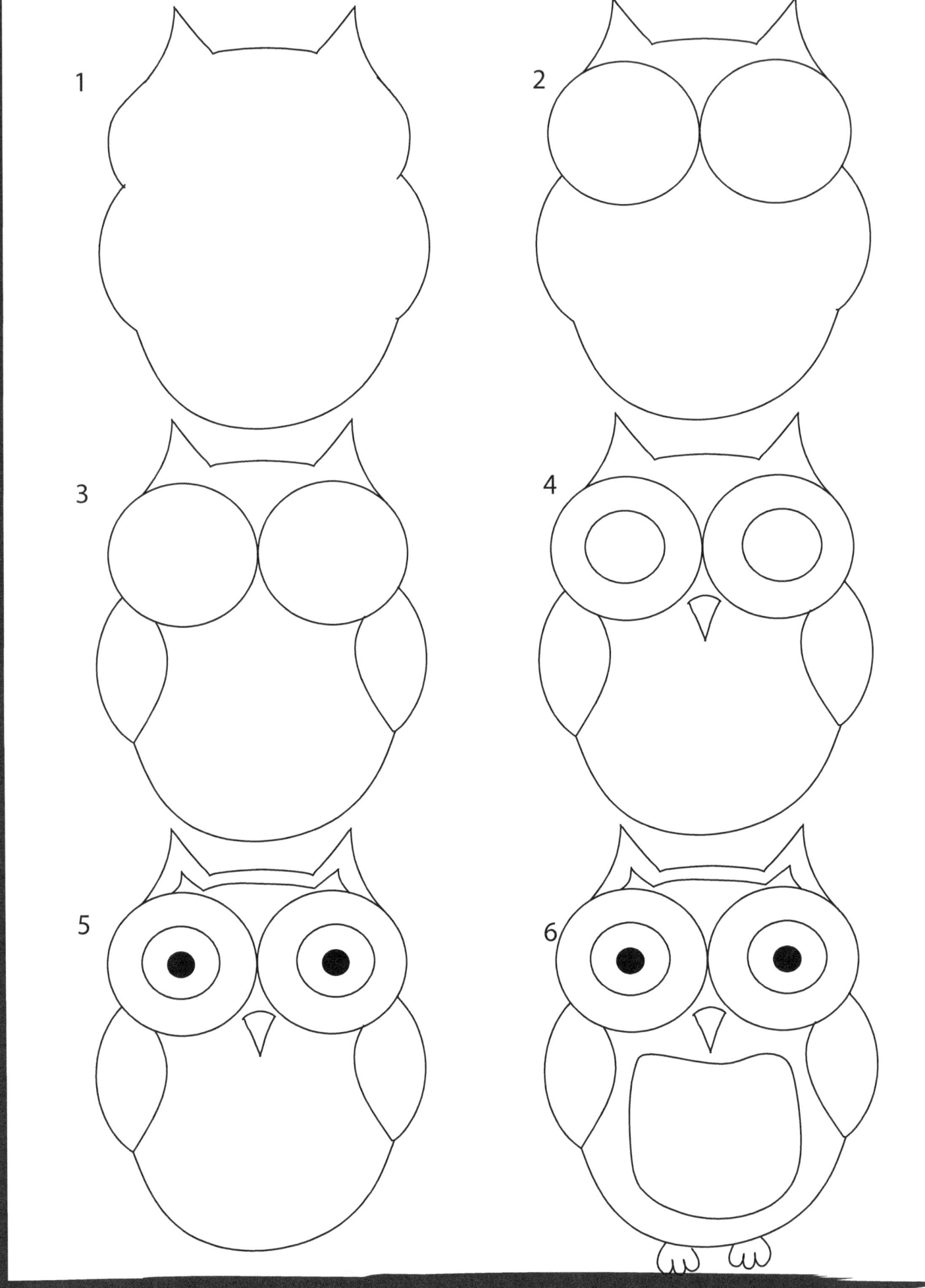

Practice Page

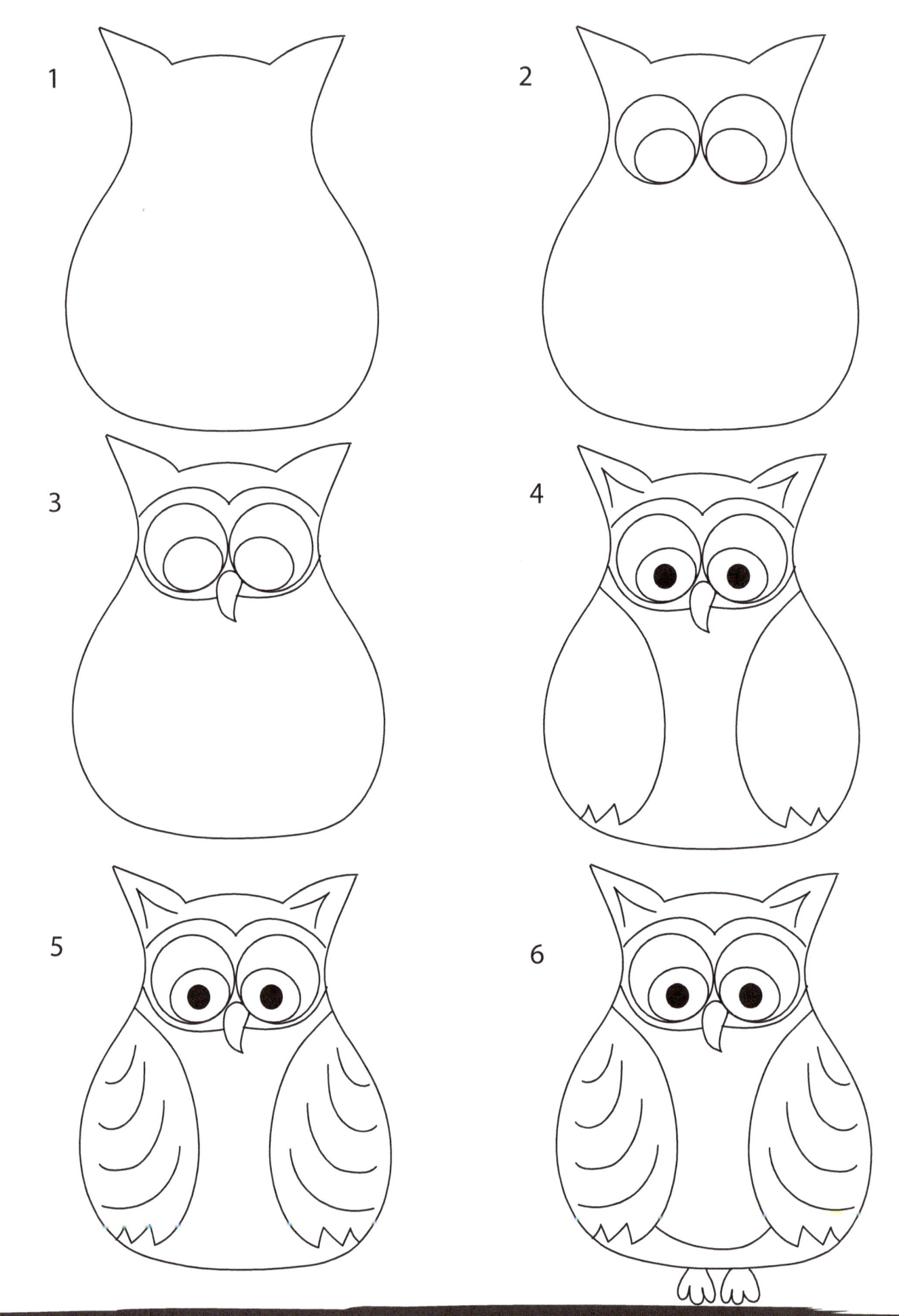

Practice Page

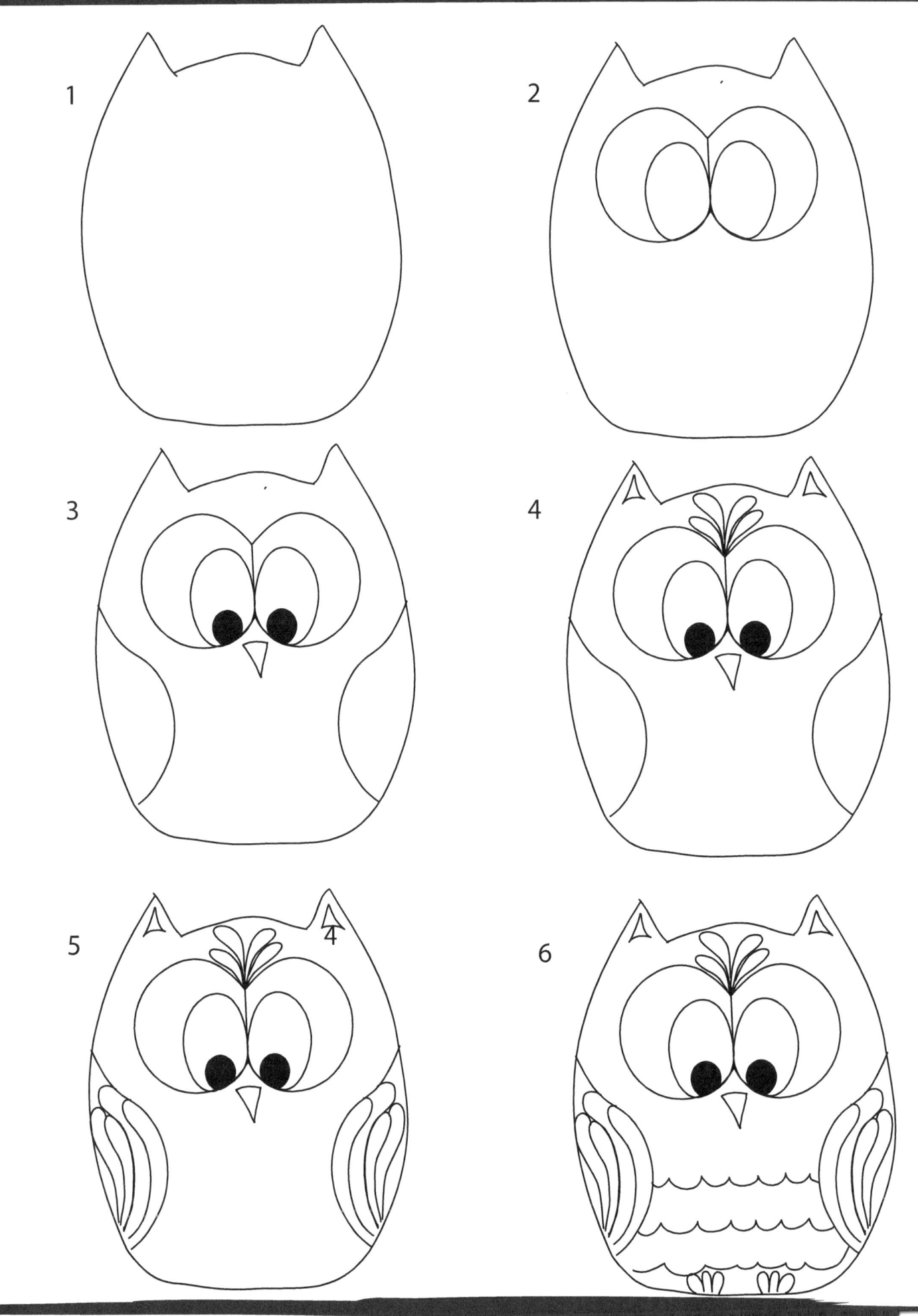

Practice Page

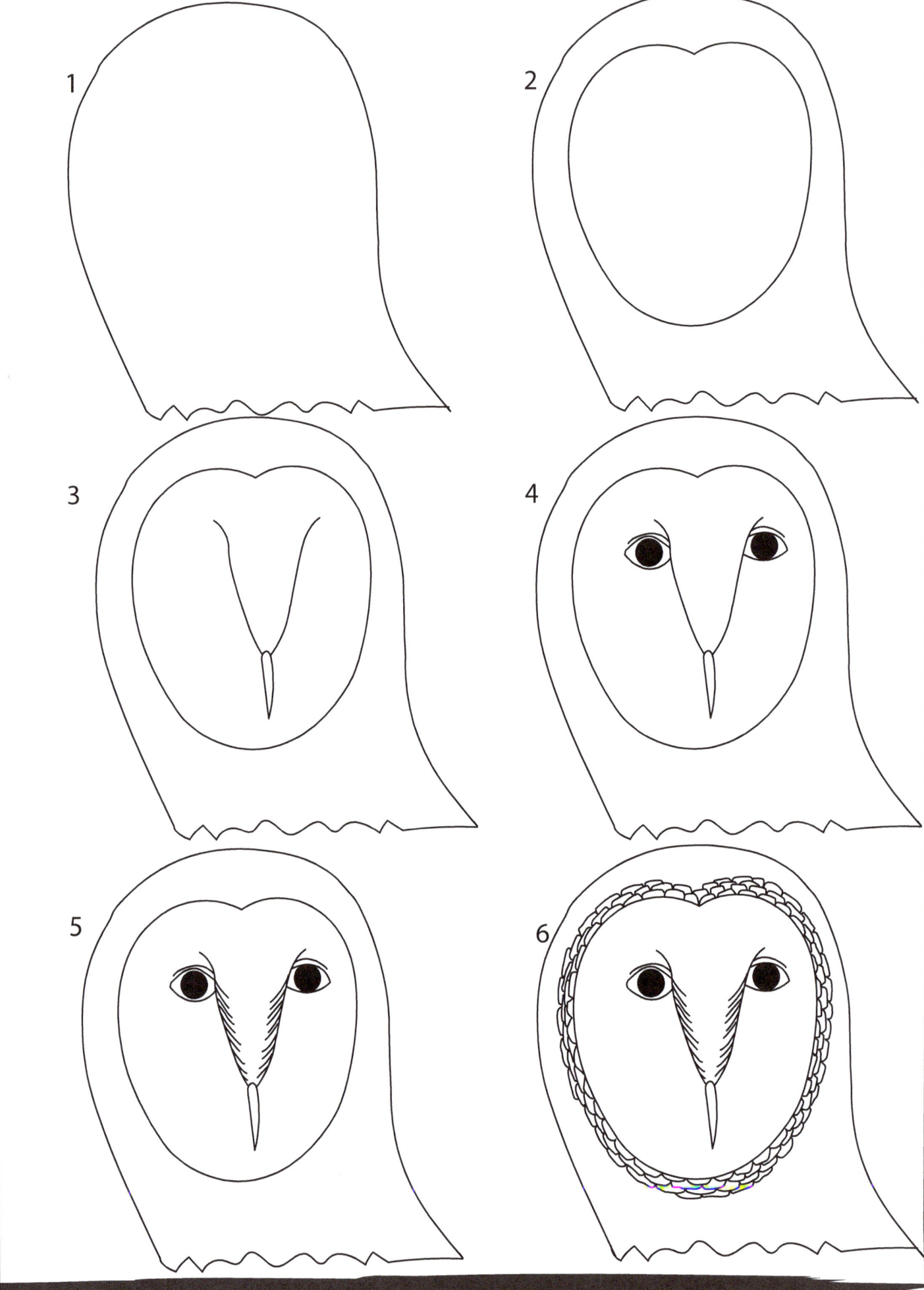

Practice Page

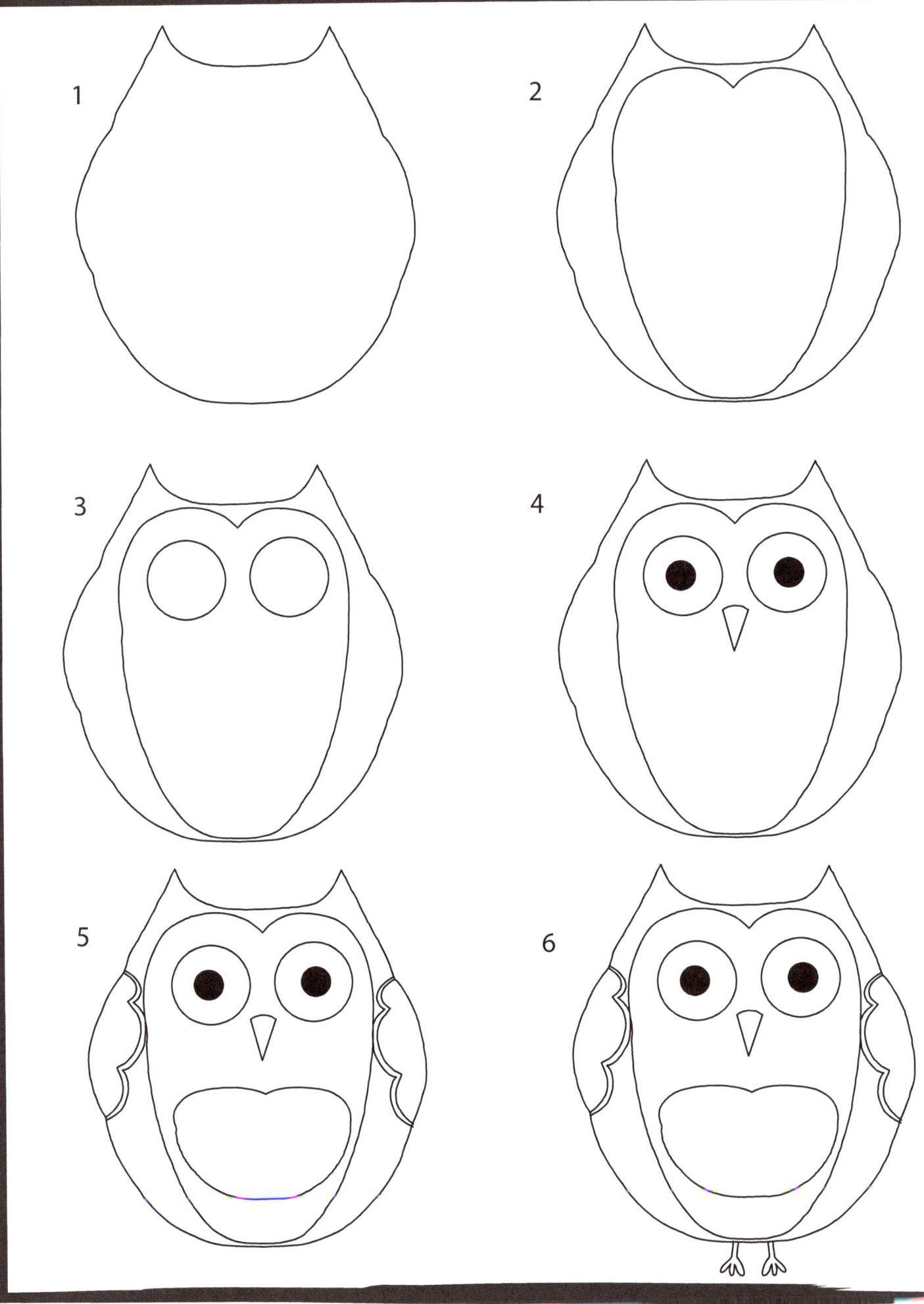

Practice Page

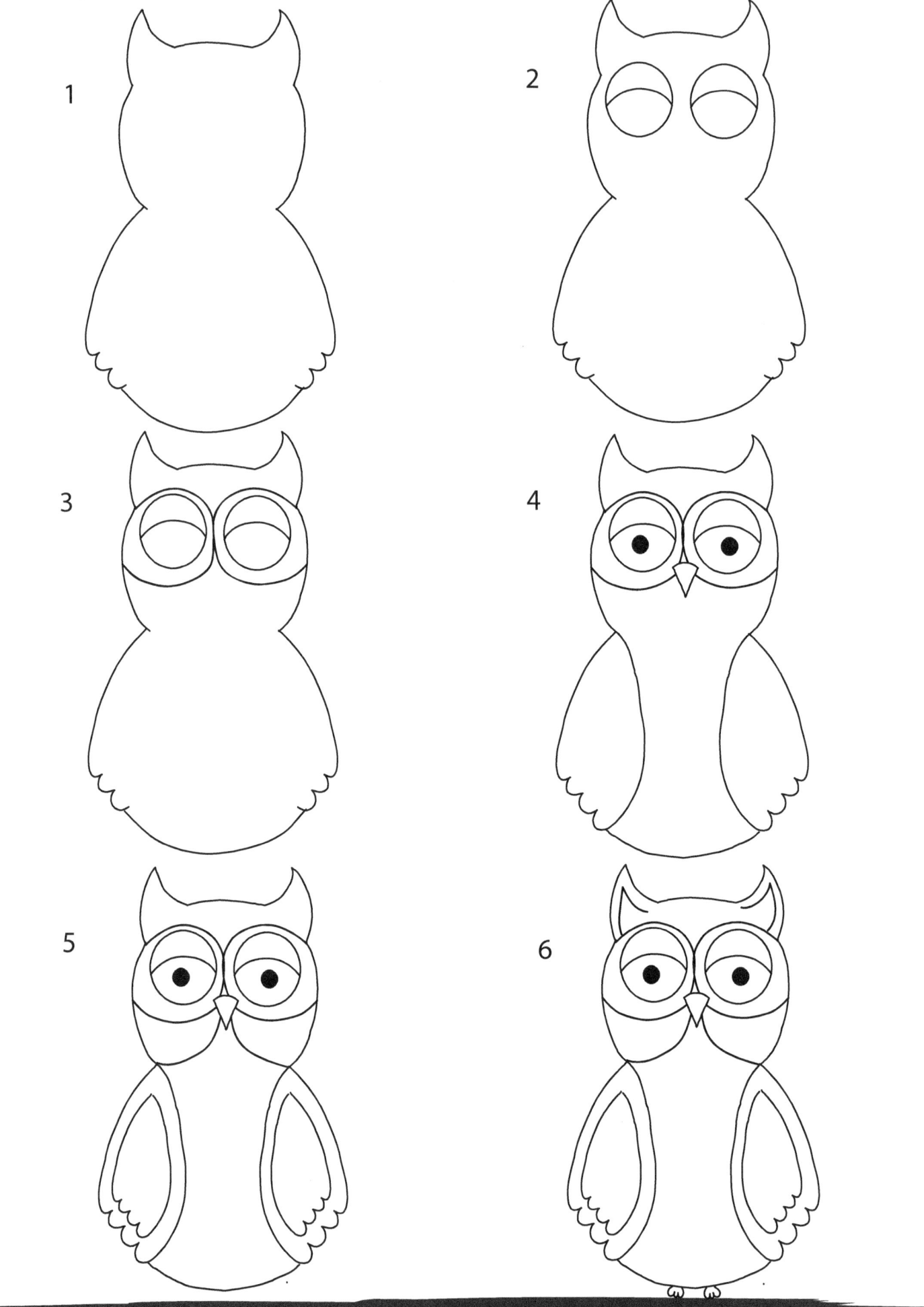

Practice Page

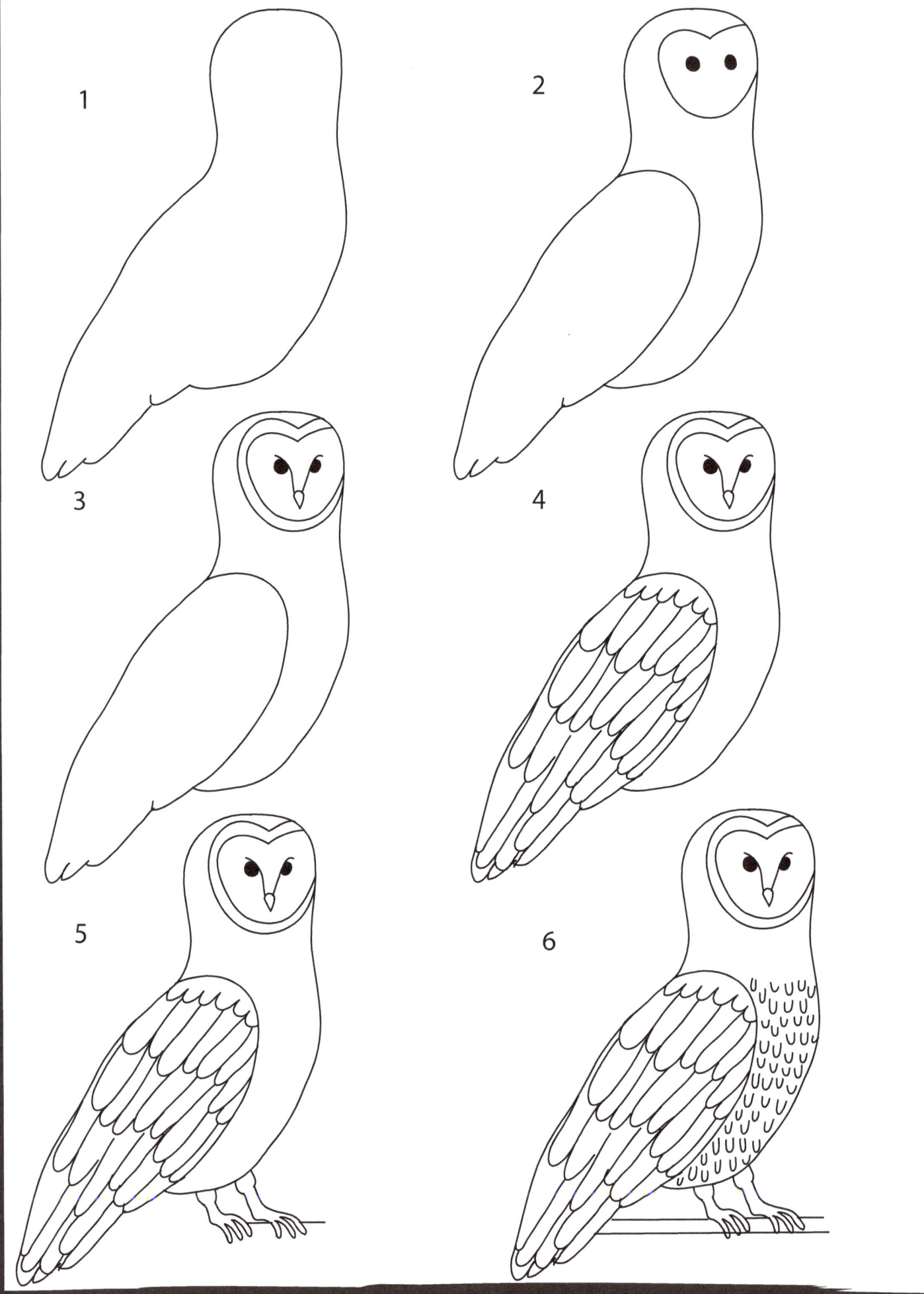

Practice Page

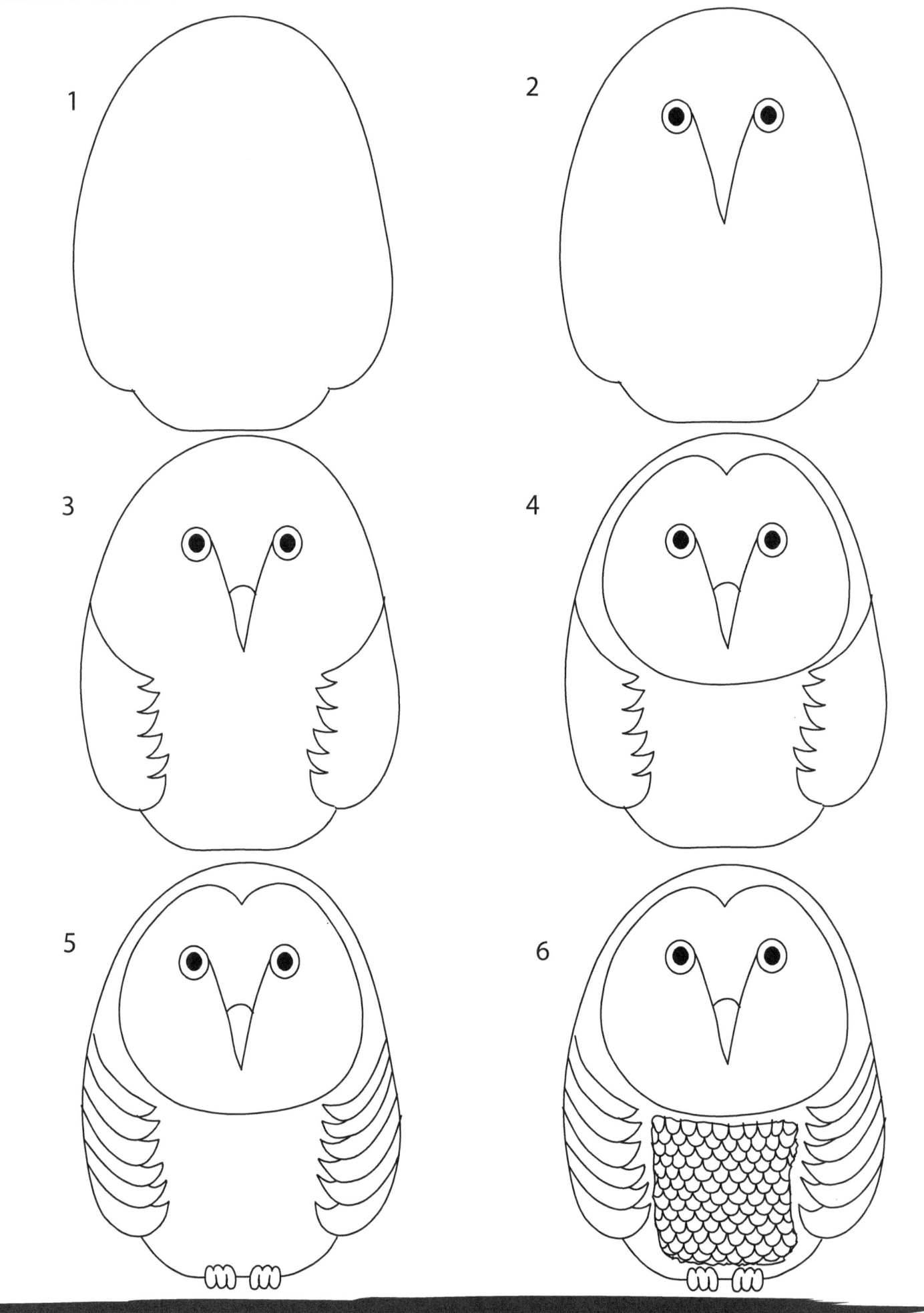

Practice Page

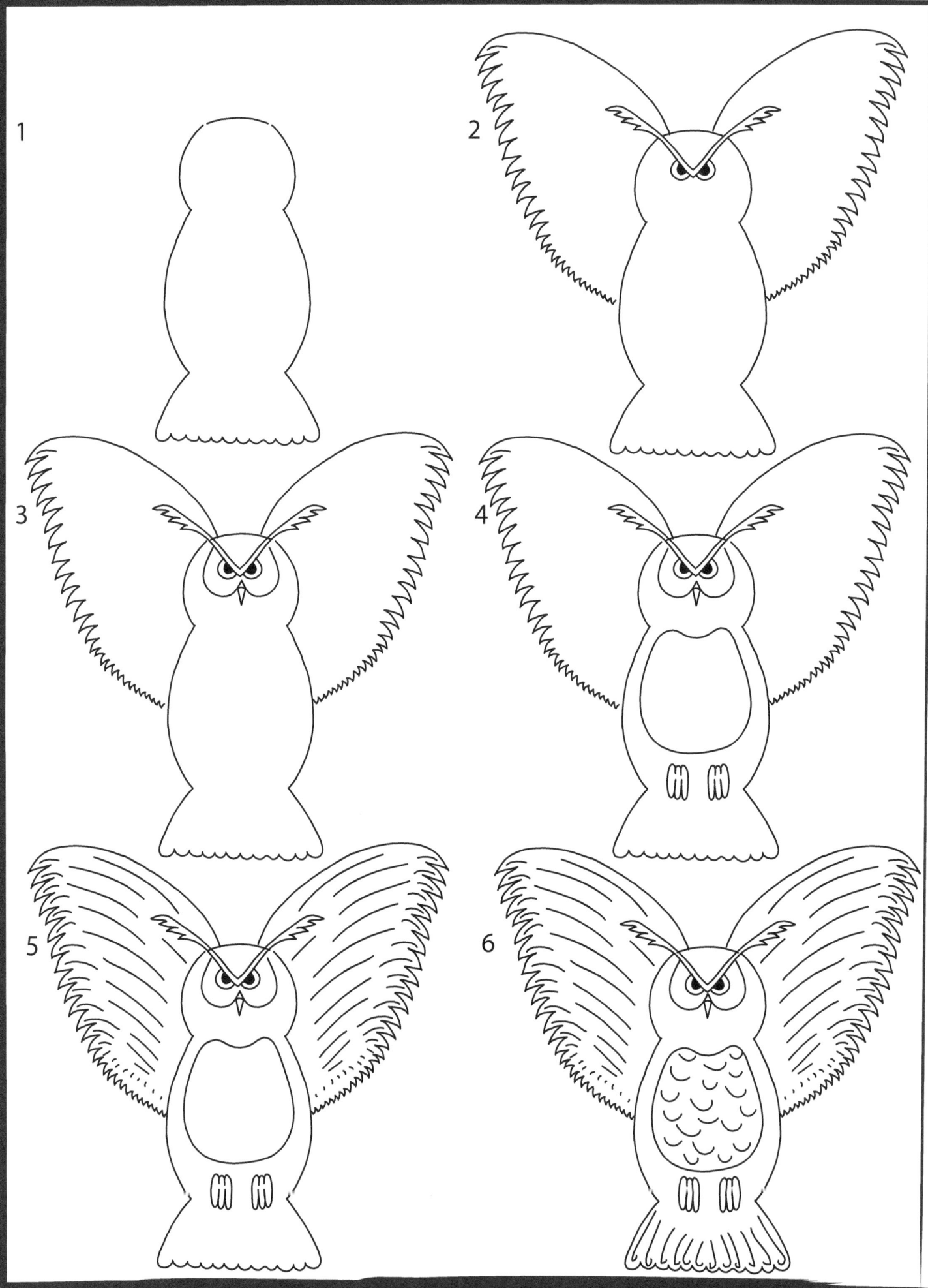

www.ingramcontent.com/pod-product-compliance
Lightning Source LLC
Chambersburg PA
CBHW062206220526
45470CB00009B/2943